THE JOY OF HEAVEN 1

Painting a Picture of Heaven

www.advbookstore.com

Written and Illustrated by

Daniel Leske

"...they shall MOUNT up with wings as eagles..." **Isaiah 40:31**

The Joy of Heaven 1: Painting a Picture of Heaven by Daniel Leske

ISBN: 978-1-59755-375-9

Published by: ADVANTAGE BOOKS™
Longwood, Florida, USA
www.advbookstore.com

Library of Congress Catalog Number: 2014948609

1

First Printing: October 2014
14 15 16 17 18 19 20 10 9 8 7 6 5 4 3 2 1
Printed in the United States of America

By writing this book, I knew the Lord had to open the door into heaven for this story to be written! As you read it, I believe that you'll be inspired by the beauty of heaven and the specialness to it!

Wings are a very special part of heaven!

Felicia is about 8 or 9 years old in stature and Wee Angel is diminutive, like her name.

I tried to paint a picture so that you can envision it!

Each person may see and feel the experience differently. As the writer, I feel that I accomplished what I set out to do!

Always remember that the Lord is the guide.

Now go with me through that doorway ------ the doorway into heaven. I hope you enjoy the story!

List of Some of the Characters

Wee Angel	She has white hair and is always a little smaller than any other angels.
Felicia	She is about 8 or 9 years old in stature with blonde hair.
Sir William	A special white winged horse.
Tuddley Teddy	A brown bear that is a friend to everyone.
Angel Michael	One of the power angels.
Zach and Barnabus	Two little bears with wings.
Jenna	A brown horse.
Sir Mark	A big white lion.
James	One of the disciples.
Berry	Another bear and a friend of Tuddley's.
Benjamin	A big elk.
Lord God Almighty	He rules heaven and earth from his throne in heaven.

Also many saints, a multitude of angels, animals and birds that are a part of the Lord's kingdom.

Chapter 1

The New Day

Felicia stood and looked at everything close at hand.

She saw tall white lilies and as she looked she saw fields of lilies moving in unison.

A gentle breeze blew past her.

She felt so much peace and she felt exuberant so she skipped about, then looked up at the sky that had big billowy clouds. As she looked, she saw something flying at a distance and it was quickly coming closer to her.

She had no fears, just knew that it was coming to see her.

Soon she knew it was an angel flying! The little one said, "Felicia, don't you know me? I'm Wee Angel! Remember me!"

"Yes, I do know you! Everything is so beautiful!"

"Isn't it wonderful here in heaven, Felicia? The Lord said you finally could come through the gate! So here you are!"

"It's so wonderful!" said Felicia. "But how......"

"Oh Felicia! It's just like being born completely new. Surely you couldn't be exactly as you were on earth. God made you all new! Now we must hurry to the special courtyard. God is waiting for you. He wants to give you wings."

"Why wings Wee Angel?"

"Oh Felicia, don't ask too many questions. Remember you had always wanted wings. Well, they are going to give you some wings. Come let's go!"

"Wee Angel, let's take some time for prayer." said Felicia.

Both prayed, praised God and thanked God. Wee Angel finished the prayer with..."Lord, thank you that I can take Felicia to some of the places in heaven."

On the two went along a golden path that had a sparkling light coming from it. The stones on the path were as though one could look right into them as one would look into water that is perfectly clear.

Felicia walked and Wee Angel flew!

Felicia had songs coming from her lips as she skipped along. She felt as light as a feather as she walked on the path.

Wee Angel was busy whistling to the songs of Felicia.

Whoosh! Something flew past Felicia.

It was another angel going to pick flowers. Shortly the angel brought them to Felicia and said, "Welcome to heaven, Felicia!"

The angel flew off as fast as the angel had come to them.

Little Felicia turned and looked in the distance.

There far away were mountains and one of them was shooting up light and fire, but not fire as she once knew! In fact, it was like a volcano, but not like a volcano.

"Oh!" laughed Wee Angel. "That mountain is doing that all the time. It can't hurt anyone, it's like a giant fountain. There's no smoke to it, no cinders as on earth."

"My, it's so beautiful Wee Angel! I've never seen anything like it."

"Oh! There's many here and much more!"

"We have many new animals that you didn't have on earth, but we'll talk about them another time."

"What's that flying?" said Felicia.

"It's a horse with wings." said Wee Angel.

DANIEL

"Oh my!" said Felicia, full of excitement. "Oh how beautiful! I know I'm going to like it here. What beauty!"

"Yes, but Felicia, I have to share something with you!" explained Wee Angel. "God told me that we must keep very busy preparing for a very, large wedding feast! He told me many guests will all be coming to heaven at one time before the major warfare."

Wee continued, "God said, 'I need all the help I can get in having it ready for our guests. They are very special! They will be coming here and making it their home.' So Felicia, we have a lot to do!"

Soon in the distance they saw a beautiful city with mansions and palaces that went as far as they could see around the base of a very large mountain with rivers, streams and many waterfalls. Everything seemed to be a definite form yet all was though light streamed from everything. The mountain had glorious colors of light. The light in areas was too bright even for the heavenly eyes. The city also carried a brightness about it! A brightness greater then anything else in the surroundings! The mountain went upwards above the city and as Felicia looked upwards, her mouth was wide open! Yet, because of the vastness, and power of glories, they could not see the top of the mountain. Both, just stood without saying one word at what they saw! Heaven, indeed was everything that Jesus said it would be! The peace was all peace. Everything was perfect.

Then Felicia started jumping up and down over its beauty.

"Oh Felicia! I told you this when you were on earth."

Felicia couldn't describe what she saw, except it was like the beauty on earth, only more of it. The trees were all perfectly straight. The waters glistened and were all pure!

She saw how light seemed to go through parts of the flowers, grass and leaves on the trees.

Wee Angel said, "Heaven is celestial, Felicia! Everything is so alive and vibrant! Everything in heaven has a glow to it! God's city is even more glowing with all its glories and power besides! It's Holy!"

The city stretched both directions. There was no dullness to the buildings since they were made with the finest gems.

Within heavenly time they slowly neared a gate to the city. On each side of the wide pathway was a pasture. Lions were laying there and sheep grazed close by, just outside the city.

“Look at that!” Felicia joyously explained, “They are together.”

“Why of course, Felicia! Why shouldn't they be! I do know what you are talking about, though!” said Wee Angel.

The gate was golden and again almost all light. Along the sides were rows and rows of roses. Felicia noticed that they had no thorns. Both sides also had rows and rows of angels going back away from, and upward as high as Felicia could see! They sang praises and hosannas to the Father, all in perfect harmony. Above the gate were colors of the rainbow, that arched upward from both sides as a gateway should be! There were streams of water flowing alongside of, and away from the wide pathway.

Wee Angel said there were many gates to the city and they were as beautiful as this one.

“Now, Felicia, you couldn't look at this gate if you were on earth because the light is so bright, but now you have heavenly eyes that can see brightness and you can look at it without it hurting you. Remember God made you perfect for heaven so that you can enjoy it as we are!”

Once inside Felicia was greeted by brothers and sisters of the Lord and hugged too! She got many hugs.

They went up and above to see Lord God.

Soon they were met by Angel Michael. Wee Angel told him that Felicia needed her wings and she needed God for them.

So he took them to Lord God and he looked at little Felicia.

“Oh Felicia,” he said, “We are so welcome to have you.”

Felicia looked at the glory of God and as he being Spirit and Light, his voice was all love to her.

Felicia said to God, “I love you..”

DANIEL

"I love you too! Can I help you, Felicia?"

"Wee Angel said I was to have wings."

God laughed and said, "Oh my child, come here." God picked her up in his arms.

"My child, your wings are there under your garments. They are still folded inside. Wee Angel, take her and get her a special garment with wing holes."

They were soon off and soon back.

Felicia said, "I can fly now!"

"Yes, my child."

"Oh God, I love you so much! I need a hug!"

God lifted Felicia up and gave her the biggest hug.

A tear came to his eye as a tear would come to his eye in heaven, "Thank you my child! Wee Angel will help show you how to fly!"

After Felicia received her hug from God, they began to look around her new home.

Chapter 2

Felicia Meets Sir William

Felicia had been flying over-under-through everything she could in heaven.

Wee Angel was there to make sure her flying didn't cause problems to others.

Felicia had her problems though! She couldn't quite get her mind to make the wings flap rather than her arms, but she got better at it.

Wee Angel told God, but he simply said, “Wee Angel, nothing to worry about! She's doing fine. Be patient and she'll soon learn.”

Once when Felicia and Wee Angel were with God, Felicia asked about Daniel.

“Oh!” God said, “Don't worry my child, he's being well watched on earth and kept busy besides. My child, you can ask me about his work once in awhile and I will talk to you. Now give me a hug, Felicia, and go your way.”

Felicia said to Wee Angel, “Now that I received wings I would like to ride one of the flying horses.”

“But Felicia,” Wee Angel quickly stated, “You don't need to ride the horses.”

“But I want too! Wee Angel. “I've got to ride one!” as she shifted back and forth on her feet.

“Let's see! We can go by Arbor Falls, they might be grazing there.” as Wee Angel pondered this.

So off they flew!

As they flew along, Felicia still bounced! She didn't fly too straight!

But fly she did, and she enjoyed it!

"Oh my, is that Arbor Falls?" as she almost flew into Wee Angel.

"Yes!" as Wee Angel flew a circle around Felicia, "See Felicia! See the beautiful fruit trees."

They were all perfect placed with the cliffs of the mountain on each side of the water as it gently fell heavenly downward into the stream. The cliffs had vines up and down on both sides of the waterfalls. All perfectly placed and all trimmed just right to the heavenly eyes.

There by the side of the stream grazed a large white horse with beautiful wings.

Wee Angel said his name was Sir William.

"He will obey you, Felicia."

Wee Angel went on, "Sir William will do whatever you ask him. All you have to do is tell him where you would like to go and he will take you there."

"That sounds so easy!" Felicia added as they flew nearer to the horse.

She had landed, but her landing was not the best as she tripped when her feet touched the soft grass.

Even the grass was of an even length, just right!

Felicia said to Wee Angel, "It's like the carpets we have on earth, but the carpets were not like this in beauty.

Wee Angel told Felicia to stoop down and smell the grass.

"Oh my! Wee Angel, what a mild, sweet fragrance. I never smelled anything like this."

Felicia hastened to say, "Nothing hurts when I do that."

"That's right, Felicia!"

Sir William continued to graze as if knowing Felicia would soon come to him.

"This is wonderful! Oh My!" Felicia couldn't stop playing on the grass.

Soon Felicia was able to give Sir William a big hug as he lowered his head towards her.

Wee Angel told Felicia to fly up on his back.

So up on his back she went, but again not the best, yet she made it.

Now Wee Angel whispered to Sir William to follow her.

Since Felicia was sitting on Sir William, Wee Angel took off flying and Sir William majestically opened his large white wings and with mighty strength followed her with Felicia on his back.

Chapter 3

Felicia and Wee Angel travel to Mighty Volcano

Felicia enjoyed her ride upon Sir William as only a child would!

As he flew over the heavenly landscape, they were not too high, because Felicia liked it that way.

However, in heaven no one could fall or got hurt as on earth. It was just that way!

Sir William turned his head, looked at his new passenger and winked at Felicia as he flew along heaven's side.

His mane of hair glistened and was far thicker than the horses on earth. Felicia was so heavenly happy! Wee Angel landed on the back of the horse.

"Where's he going?" asked Felicia.

"I told him to take us to the Mighty Volcano you saw before!"

Felicia was wondering, "We won't get hurt there, will we?"

"No one can get hurt." as Wee Angel pointed to different sights of trees, fields of flowers, streams and some animals Felicia hadn't seen before!

She went on, "We can go so close to enjoy it, but then we just know that's as far as we go! Besides, it's not like the volcanoes on earth. It's more like a giant fountain for beauty, majesty, and a special gift by God for us to enjoy. Remember, it's not the only one. There are many here."

As Sir William flew closer, the two were astounded at it's beauty.

High – high – high into the heaven-o-sphere the fire-like waters arose.

Then gently, very gently the fire-like waters came down and so softly drifted as in a perfect pattern to the sides of the mountain down into a stream and went over a falls into a pool which slowly moved back into the mountain. Felicia could not get over how slow the lava(not like earth's) came downward, just like a falling feather.

There were not any bad odors or smoke, in fact it smelled so pleasing!

As Felicia and Wee Angel watched from the back of Sir William who had landed, while saints were watching and talking as well!

Many brothers and sisters were in heaven. They enjoyed and talked about God's beautiful creation.

"Sometime I'll tell you, and show you, one of God's special sanctuaries where his brothers and sisters come to worship him. Remember, that in this kingdom of heaven, not everyone that comes to heaven can come to!"

"This is the highest mansion of heaven and most special because of it's closeness to God's City.

The scripture tells us, 'Blessed are the pure in heart for they shall see God.' We can go to their mansions, but they cannot come into this mansion. It's just that way! Oh! They have beauties of their mansions that are beyond all comparison. Only the highest of God's chosen are here. God said he would have a people unto himself."

Wee Angel went on, "Even though this mansion is so special, it is not the biggest place in heaven. That's because it's so special, but do remember a lot of horses have wings and it's plenty big as compared to earth."

As they stood, Felicia groomed Sir William, and then he would put his head close to her so she could rub him behind the ears.

Every now and then he whinnied and acted so proud of his two little passengers.

He wanted everyone to know who he was helping out!

Wee Angel and Felicia looked at all the mountains to the sides of Mighty Volcano. Felicia saw they had snow on their peaks and beautiful streams, that slowly meandered around and by the mountains.

Wee Angel in her excitement about everything spoke, "We'll come back again!"

They prayed and thanked God for what they had seen, conversed, and then shouted with heavenly love the fun they were having in heaven.

Felicia used her wings to fly back up on Sir William's back. Wee Angel, after flying over a few trees, joined her. She nodded to Sir William.

Off! Over a river they flew on more adventures in heaven!

Chapter 4

Meeting Sir Mark

Sir William landed with Wee Angel and Felicia hanging on to special hair that God had so created on the horse just for them to be comfortable. The horses in heaven were shaped just right over the back so one sat in total safety as the horse flew in the heavenly sky.

They had been flying over valleys, past hills, over streams and trees of all varieties and colors, Even the trunks of the trees were colorful and had no drabness, but not as bright as the leaves.

Felicia wondered why they had stopped! She enjoyed everything so much!

Wee Angel said, "I think Sir William wants you to meet a friend of his."

They were in a very flowered meadow, with birds busy about their work and were singing much the same as on earth.

Wee Angel said, "Their eating habits are different since no bugs exist in heaven. The birds eat seeds. God has some small creations like a bug, but they never will bother you and they will only be in certain regions."

Before more could be done or seen they heard a roar of a friendly greeting.

Then slowly walking out of the forest was a very big lion. He had the most beautiful white color with a grayish mane. Wee Angel immediately flew over to him and rode on his back as he walked closer to Sir William and Felicia.

"My! He's big and he's beautiful!" exclaimed Felicia.

Wee Angel flew all around him and clapped her little hands.

Every once in a while she said, "Praise the Lord!" and other heavenly words came forth!

He was close to Sir William and they seemed to just enjoy being there. Many times while Sir William was grazing, Sir Mark was close by, laying and just plain resting as most lions like to do! Sir William always liked his company.

Felicia looked at the heavenly tall trees he had walked out of earlier. There were taller than any tree she had seen on earth.

As they stood there a gentle mist was falling all around them. A mist that gently fell and watered the plants and trees.

They stood there and enjoyed it, and it felt so pleasant to them. Felicia asked Wee Angel about the clouds mist.

"Oh Felicia! You ask questions just like I ask God. I'm always asking him about his creation, especially since I saw earth, and I've seen the differences between them."

She continued, "God told me in his own way that the clouds in heaven are much higher than on earth. By this, storms cannot occur. The sky in heaven is such that everything appears to float, and the mist comes down much gentler than on earth. God has an element in the sky in heaven that keeps the droplets smaller in size for this gentleness. Now that you've seen how plush everything is in heaven. Well, God said that here in heaven there is also an element in heaven's land. He calls it, ah! I can't remember it's name. It knows exactly how much water each variety of plant needs. It's a fancy name, but he said that this is how it works to keep everything looking so nice. Remember, he said he knows the very hairs on your head, as well as each plant, the trees, and the shrubs, the vines, the vegetables, and fruits."

"My!" Felicia said.

Wee Angel added, "As you look into the skies, they are a richer blue than on earth."

Felicia asked, "Can I talk to you more about these things?"

"I think you will ask no matter what, Felicia. You are just like me in questions." Wee Angel joyfully answered as she quickly flew up to a tree limb to sit!

They noticed that Sir William and Sir Mark had walked away to lay down by a tall tree. Other lions had come by, as well as a hawk, elephant, some buffalo and even some prairie dogs barked in the distance.

Both Felicia and Wee Angel saw some large strawberries so they just had to have some of them.

A short distance away was an orange tree, so Wee Angel flew over, picked off a couple, and brought them back for Felicia and her to eat.

As with all fruits and berries in heaven. They were sweetened just right to the taste.

"Wow!" Felicia said as she took a bite of the strawberry. "My! Oh my!"

In the far distance were some mountains, and between them and the mountains, were some beautiful hills.

There were always golden paths. They were just a part of the planning.

They went through the meadows, forests, by streams, rivers, and through fields of flowers.

Here brothers and sisters of heaven could walk or if riding flying horses, they could land with ease!

Little Felicia, hugged Sir Mark as best she could!

She held tight to his beautiful mane. Sir Mark smiled as a lion would smile and Felicia whispered into his ear, "I love you. Please let me see you again."

Wee Angel said as she was all smiles, "Felicia, you can see him anytime. We'll come back."

After Wee Angel and Felicia were on the back of Sir William. He gently opened his powerful wings and they were off again looking at heaven.

Felicia called out to Sir Mark, "We'll be back, Sir Mark!"

Chapter 5

On to a Special Lake

Wee Angel and Felicia were busy enjoying the overlook of heaven's land from the back of Sir William.

The large white horse with wings was quietly flying towards a special lake.

As he flew, he was so quiet, but Wee Angel and Felicia were busy talking as usual. It seemed they loved to talk and so talk, they did!

Felicia didn't have any special questions, but just kept talking! She enjoyed herself so much!

Felicia couldn't remember any of her problems that she had on earth. They were all taken away from her.

Wee Angel and Felicia talked about many of the sisters and brothers, they had met along the paths at some of the stops. There were Ernie, Vicky, Terrance, Marty, Fred, Allan, Mark, Mary, Jane, Shirley, and many, many more!

There maybe were some that you even knew!

Sir William kept flying onward. The gracefulness of the flying horse in flight is awesome.

As he flew along a mallard duck came flying to them and perched almost on the tail. This sometimes happened with the flying horses that they would have a guest or two, but they loved it!

He seemed to enjoy the ride. As on earth, he kept saying, "Quack, Quack!""

Wee Angel would point to other horses with passengers as they flew to their destinations. If close they waved to them.

Many times they saw others praising and worshiping God on golden paths, or even as they were, on the back of horses.

Soon they saw a large golden lake. Yes golden!

“Oh my!” Felicia said again, “Golden, a golden lake!”

The waters appeared gold in color.

Soon they came to it's shore and Sir William landed right on the shoreline.

The waters were perfectly clear and they saw fish swimming, but the water looked golden in color. The shoreline had pebbles and sand of all colors of browns to dark golden. They could barely see the shore on the other side. It was so wide.

Felicia, of course, had to go out in the water. Wee Angel joined her and so did Sir William.

The three of them walked in the water.

Sir William, of course, had to have a drink of it, as all horses would!

Felicia cupped up the water in her hands and splashed it in her face. The water was nice and warm for them.

They saw the pebbles on the bottom of Golden Lake as Wee Angel called it, as they looked way out into the waters since it was so clear.

The splashing wasn't enough for Felicia. She went into the water as far as she could and enjoyed it completely.

Wee Angel splashed some of the water on Sir William.

Felicia kept saying to Wee Angel, “A lake where the water is actually golden!”

“It's so wonderful! Thank you Lord for your heaven. Thank you!” prayed Felicia.

Both stood in prayer and thanked our Lord for everything they had seen, for his thoughtfulness in caring so much for others, and them.

"In heaven, there is a reverence to everything you see, and to everything that happens, Felicia." softly spoke Wee Angel. "Everything praises God or shows praise to him in its mannerisms and movement."

It wasn't too long and another large angel came to them. He said to Wee Angel that she was to bring Felicia to God when she could get there.

The larger angel left quickly as he bid the two and Sir William good-day(In heaven it is always good-day.)

The two walked and walked along the shore, picked up the pebbles and tossed them.

Sir William followed, of course!

Gentle rolling hills were around the lake with plenty of flowers, groupings of trees, and shrubs. There were lavender colors of flowers, white daises, irises, orchids, some patches of tulips, roses as well, and many more.

There were apple trees still filled with white blossoms which stayed that way all the time just to enjoy!

The grass was even and again looked like a beautiful carpet. In the trees, the birds sang, and on the lake were many kinds of ducks and geese. There was special harmony and purity to all the sounds that each made as the two listened and talked about it.

The honking geese made its beautiful honk as well!

Wee Angel was still busy splashing and washing Sir William.

Though soon they were ready to go! Off they rode on the back of Sir William as he flew so they could see God!

Chapter 6

Their First Visit to Angel Choir Practice

Felicia and Wee Angel got off of Sir William at the gate of the court to God's Throne. They gave Sir William a big hug and told him they would be out in a short time.

Once inside they walked up to God's Throne as they were escorted by several angels.

God said, "Come closer children. I wanted to see how you were doing!"

Felicia spoke up and said, "Lord, I'm doing fine. Wee Angel has been so good and showing me many places."

Wee Angel told God about the places they had been, including Golden Lake.

Lord God said to them, "Now Wee Angel take Felicia to one of our choir practices. I'm quite sure Felicia will enjoy that!"

"Can we have a hug, God?"

"Oh yes!" Lord God kindly spoke and lifted both up at the same time, gave them a big hug, and gently down again on their feet.

They thanked Lord God and slowly walked back to Sir William. On the way out of the courtyard, they walked past two brothers. Felicia recognized them as being evangelists on earth. They greeted each other and then they went out the gate to Sir William.

Once outside, they saw one of the higher positioned angels with Sir William and another horse.

The angel said he needed Sir William, but he was told where Wee Angel and Felicia were going, so he brought them, Jenna. She was a large brown horse with a deeper brown mane.

Jenna didn't have wings, but the angel said the choir singing was not far away from there.

Wee Angel and Felicia said their good-days to Sir William and greeted Jenna as in heaven everyone is polite. They just are!

Both got unto the back of Jenna (one climbed and the other flew) and directed her on a path towards the choir grounds.

As they were riding on Jenna, there were others headed towards the grounds. Some on horses, some walked, and as you know some by heavenly sky, as all angels have wings, and some of those like Felicia that were given wings by God.

Wee Angel said to Felicia, "Those wings are an honor and very special. Not everyone gets them. The wings are very vital to the Trinity in God's creation."

"Wee Angel, thank you for telling me." softly spoke Felicia with tears in her eyes.

Felicia continued, "Can you tell me where Jesus is right now?"

"Oh yes," said Wee Angel. "He's very busy as he still is a part of God. Remember he greeted you when you came to heaven."

She continued as they walked along the path, "He has the largest marriage coming up very shortly. He has the largest feast to prepare for his people. The largest grouping of his angels. The largest celebration in heaven and very shortly after the largest war on earth. The end of the devil's torment and power. Remember in Psalm 23 where David said, ***'Thou preparest a table before me in the presence of mine enemies***.'"

"Felicia," Wee Angel went on, "The angels such as Michael, Gabriel, Raphael that you know about and others like Kingstiel, Markiel keep saying to God, 'Lets take care of the dragon now and get rid of him now.' They get impatient, so you see God is extremely busy with everything. A little thought, Felicia, the red dragon is the devil at full armor. This is his armor in time of war. That's why he's talked about in Revelation."

"Now remember this seven years is his total power on earth. After the Rapture, the red dragon will make appearances on earth so that people can see him. There will be other things he will do during this time and it's a part of his great deception, but I'll tell you another time. The red dragon will take it out on the people because of the celebration and feast going on in heaven."

"My Wee Angel, I'm glad I'm here."

"Felicia, you and I and many others will be helping the Lord get everything just right for this feast, so you will have some work to do!"

Felicia humbly answered, "I feel so honored I can help for those coming!"

Jenna was going down a slope of the hillside. Beautiful yellow flowers were on each side and some evergreen trees on the left side. Jenna waited on special grounds.

Once past a curve of some small hills and inside, they saw many benches. They were not benches as we know, but wood that had grown or a tree that grew to make a bench form, covered with something very heavenly special for comfort like a cushion.

The benches were filled with brothers and sisters waiting for the angels to sing to them.

The horses grazed on special grounds outside the outdoor sanctuary.

There are many-many sanctuaries in heaven!

This was one of the smaller ones.

Felicia and Wee Angel took a seat and waited for the choir.

The seats seemed to go for miles. All out in a pasture-like land with some deer grazing with trees to the outside of the seats and also streams of water flowed very slowly away from and around the sanctuary. In the distance were some mountains. These were very bluish in color, there were rainbows above, and some waterfalls that never went away!

Even in the sanctuary or amongst the seats were little tiny flowers, pretty whites, pinks, purples, and yellows.

Felicia said, “They are so little.”

And high above the sanctuary and seats, even the clouds formed an arched roof to the grounds. They were very light and feathery.

Soon the angels came from all directions and flew to their places for singing.

They hovered in the air making up many tiers all around the sides of the seats. There were thousands of angels.

All were in rows just as a choir would be! In big meetings it could be thousands upon thousands upon thousands of angels.

Then the leading angel hovered above the seats and directed them in song and praise of Lord God Almighty.

“Some of the songs,” Wee Angel said to Felicia, “you sang on earth and some are new.”

Felicia sat with tears of joy. She couldn't stop crying, she was so happy.

Wee Angel gave her, a big hug and said, “Felicia, we knew you would be so happy and grateful.”

Others that had just come to heaven were the same way, totally amazed by everything they saw there.

As it finished, Felicia and Wee Angel greeted others who were there at the choir practice. They were there because God allowed them to come to heaven.

Chapter 7

Felicia and Wee Angel Finally Meet Tuddley Teddy

Wee Angel and Felicia left the choir practice and soon with Jenna were walking along a path on the other side of the open air sanctuary. They walked towards the mountains.

Two sisters, two brothers, and a couple of children walked with them for a ways. Martha, Joyce, Jim, Terry and the children were Robin and Annette.

They talked about the beautiful singing by the angels and the beauty around them. They were all so filled with joy and high emotions. Remember this was heaven and they don't get sad! Felicia and Wee Angel started to get tired, so they told the others they had to rest someplace.

The others went on, but Felicia, Wee Angel, and Jenna went to a small grouping of fruit trees along the path.

There were some peaches on one of them and a fruit Felicia hadn't seen before on another tree. Of course, they had to take one of each and sat at the base of the tree.

Even the base of the tree was different in heaven. God had again grown little flowers with stems that were just like a cushion.

Jenna stood and grazed within distance as Felicia and Wee Angel rested, and soon they went to sleep!

Both were very tired! The fruit was half eaten, fell from their hands to the heavenly land by their sides.

Soon some antelope and a couple of cougars came and walked past them to the stream. It didn't seem to bother, Felicia and Wee Angel. They slept on!

Within heaven's time, they woke up from their rest and talked about how young everyone looked in heaven.

Wee Angel said to Felicia, "Our bodies have more light in them. Light doesn't age. Again this is a gift from Jesus.

Some cows, a few horses, and even a giraffe came past Felicia and Wee Angel. Egrets, some swans and a few beaver were in the stream.

They had seen many kinds of animals and birds. One couldn't name them all! They were free to roam and be pets to everybody there.

Wee Angel and Felicia talked for a long time. They looked across the stream to the benches and hillside. They saw more meadows and grasslands with groupings of trees placed just right by God.

The golden path had other paths coming unto it from other directions. Some led to forested areas, others to areas of flowers, others to some small hill regions, and others to the mountains.

They barely got started traveling when a brown bear came along side of them.

Wee Angel knew the bear and had many times sat on his back.

Everybody called him, Tuddley Teddy.

He was so cuddly that he earned his name, besides children when saying cuddly often the word came out tuddly. He always lived up to the name given him.

Tuddley Teddy went up to Felicia and wanted a big hug. So Felicia hugged his head and put her arms around his neck as best she could!

He wanted to follow along with them, so follow along with them he did!

It seemed none of them were in any hurry so they often stopped and sat by the stream.

Of course, Tuddley Teddy found a berry bush close by and he ate as many berries as he could get down while they played in the stream.

The Joy of Heaven 1

Felicia said to Wee Angel, “All of the fruits and berries are so much bigger here and sweeter too!”

Soon they saw flying towards them the most beautiful sights!

“Look at them!” said Felicia, “Look at them!”

They flew around and around Tuddley. They were two small bears with wings, about the size of bear cubs on earth.

Wee Angel said, “That's Zach and Barnabus! They are close friends to Tuddley.”

Zach was a little darker brown. Barnabus was a golden brown.

Both flew around Tuddley, Felicia, and Wee Angel.

They soon stood and greeted them.

“Small bears with wings.” said Felicia.

Wee Angel answered, “There's many like them. That's their size! I know some of their names. There's Zek, Winta(a white bear), Faithful, Crystal, Joy and many others! They know Tuddley.”

Soon the good-days were said and the two flew away in the heavenly sky. Tuddley wiggled all over with excitement.

Felicia said, “They're awesome!”

“There's a special waterfall where I want to take you.” said Wee Angel. “You could see part of it when we were sitting at the choir practice. There's no hurry though, to get to the falls.”

Felicia relaxed with her feet in the water. It was the prettiest blue and many of the stones under the water sparkled like they were on fire. Other stones along the stream bed were as colored glass.

As they sat, a mist from the very high clouds came down so gently over God's heavenly lands. It was so gentle and fine that it felt so comfortable to the both of them.

The mist never lasted too long, just long enough for everything to stay plush and green.

There were no dead sticks, dead plants, or anything that suggested death, as there was no death in heaven, only life.

Soon Tuddley Teddy was full and the four were walking in the mountains.

Chapter 8

The Falls and a Special Room

They walked through some trees and overhanging plants along the path. The slopes of the mountains rose quite sharply! They continued to walk along the path which went along the stream getting more and more into the high mountains. The mountains took on a bluish hue as you looked at them. As they walked they came to a ridge with a lookout where they could look back and see the many seats of the outdoor sanctuary.

"Oh what a view!" said Felicia in total awe! "Look at all the yellow hues above the pastures in the sky."

"Felicia, that's a part of God's glory!" added Wee Angel.

One saw the thousands of seats, the high ceiling made by the clouds, also the streams, and trees.

Between the seats and the high roof of clouds were the prettiest yellow to golden tones.

Felicia asked Wee Angel, "How come we couldn't see that when we sat in the seats. There we saw the beautiful blues above.

Wee Angel laughed, "Felicia, that's God and heaven. From one direction you can see beautiful hues and from the other direction the colors can change when looking at the heavenly sky."

She went on, "Remember, Felicia, God is up here and his glory shines all over the heavenly lands. Powerful glory! Sometimes it's very soft and another time very radiant, but always pleasing to our heavenly eyes. Beauty to behold!"

DANIEL

Tuddley Teddy was trying to climb up a tree, and both Wee Angel and Felicia took hold of his fur to let him know they were going! Tuddley Teddy decided to follow them for a while yet! Jenna, the beautiful brown horse was always by them.

Felicia again had tears of joy, for her little heavenly heart could not contain all that she was seeing there.

Onward, they walked along the mountains golden path to the falls.

At the falls, they stood on a large flat platform of a solid rock. Felicia looked upward and saw at the very top, the mountain was in the cloud cover. The water slowly fell down to the first level, then outward, and fell to the base.

The stream was not an extremely large stream, but the height of each falls was greater than any falls on earth. Around the falls at the top up by the clouds were three separate rainbows. The rainbows always stayed there and the falls never lessened or increased in its flow to the stream.

On each level were trees on each side of the stream.

They looked through a very narrow opening between mountains, and saw more heavenly lands on the other side of the mountains.

Wee Angel said they would go to those lands another time. Remember the land in heaven is not made the same way as the land on earth.

The narrow passage through the mountains to this land reminded Felicia of the eye of the needle that Jesus talked about in his Word.

Felicia also saw high spires of rock formations that looked like the spires on a church.

At the base of the falls were large pools. The rocks were so formed so the water flowed gently over several steps of rock before it went into the stream.

From the platform there was a rock bridge across the stream, to the other side. On the other side of the stream was a small rock formed entrance into a special room.

Inside the rocked formed room was a special waterfall that made sounds like music as the water gently flowed over some rocks into a stream. It made this special sound like musical notes. The doorway to the special room was between two large rocks and Felicia saw an openness past the rocks with openness above, yet all surrounded by the rock mountains so that there was only one entrance.

Two angels were sitting on a smaller rock by the entrance.

Felicia sensed something very special about the area.

It was like a side of the mountain was cut out and enough open space for this room, and an opening to its upper side to the heavenly sky for light.

Also along the bed of the stream was a huge olive tree.

Wee Angel said to Felicia, "God said that the olive tree was older than any tree on earth."

Felicia looked at it with respect thinking of the tree planted by the waters mentioned in the Bible.

Wee Angel and Felicia climbed aboard Jenna and they walked back along the trail with Tuddley Teddy following close behind them.

Felicia thought about where they sat at choir practice miles away, as they could see the mountain in the distance and the falls from the sanctuary.

She looked at a rock mountain with a special room of God's.

Chapter 9

To the Sea

Wee Angel and Felicia upon Jenna, and also Tuddley Teddy left the mountains and were again along the stream somewhat close to where they had met Tuddley Teddy. Felicia and Wee Angel flew off by some trees. They could tell Tuddley Teddy was looking for a nap.

They played games with Tuddley, jumping on and off his back. Something like tag, only Tuddley was more of a hurdle.

Tuddley's nose touched Wee Angel's cheek. It was his way to give them a kiss and say how much he loved them.

Wee Angel said, “Felicia, it's time for Tuddley to nap longer! We'll see him again!”

Felicia and Wee Angel gave him another hug and then, Tuddley Teddy climbed up into one of the trees for his long nap.

They napped again at the foot of the tree, but soon they woke as a couple more saints of heaven: Jim, Karen, Barb, and others walked past them. They greeted Wee Angel and Felicia. They hugged them too!

Wee Angel climbed upon Jenna and took a path that headed away from the stream.

Within time, they came to some small, rolling hills, and there grazing was Sir William.

Wee Angel told Felicia about a very large sea they could reach with Sir William.

They said their good-days to Jenna with their hugs and both climbed this time upon Sir William's back.

Soon they were in the air flying to a very large sea.

As Sir William flew along, Wee Angel and Felicia looked at heaven's land, saw many brothers and sisters below them. Many angels in flight as well! For Felicia seeing the angels in flight was awesome!

Everyone they met was so filled with joy and so very happy. They talked about God, about Jesus, and the Holy Spirit, plus all of God's creation.

Felicia asked Wee Angel, "Where are the disciples and others from the Bible?"

Wee Angel answered, "Now, Felicia, everyone that comes here wants to see those that were in the Bible. God has to be a little protective of them, so they are seen and visited with by everyone, but in his time. You'll meet them, Felicia, be patient."

Soon they landed on the edge of the sea.

They looked as far as the eye could see and saw no land, just the most beautiful water.

"What is its name, Wee Angel?"

"Oh, it's the Sea of Galilee, just as on earth, but much bigger." said Wee Angel.

The waters were the most beautiful turquoise blues. The water looked like it had a glory all its own!

Like it had a huge light within the water, plus it had such a glow to it as both looked and looked at the sea.

The waters were so calm. The sands of the shoreline were a color between white and light brown. Again the little grains of sand glistened and sparkled. Not too bright, just right, and it was pleasing to the eyes.

Along the shore, outside the sanded areas were beautiful straight tall trees.

The greens of the leaves were very high off the heaven's land. As one looked, one saw the tall trunks, straight, going high above with the crown or greens of the trees high up above them.

Between the trees, were beautiful rocks, shrubs, and flowers of various colors that made the scene complete.

The birds were singing their songs.

As far as they could see in both directions, Wee Angel and Felicia saw these, extremely tall, trees along the sanded shoreline of the Sea of Galilee.

In one direction, they saw way...... way, away, some mountains close by the sea and they were a greenish hue so they must have been covered with trees.

Wee Angel, Felicia and Sir William could not get enough of this special sea.

Everything was perfect!

Chapter 10

To the Pond

Wee Angel said to Felicia, "Come, let's follow the path into the woods. We can walk for a while! So onto a path they walked into the woods that went along this serene sea.

They walked and walked, talked and talked! Sir William, of course, followed them, as well! As they walked, they listened to the birds in the trees.

The tops of the trees were very high off heaven's land, but that didn't bother the birds at all! They sang songs of majesty.

Felicia said, "Wee Angel, when the birds sing at times it's like they burst out into a special singing of praises to our Father."

Wee Angel answered, "I wondered how long before you would notice that! They sing and chirp as all birds do, but at times they sing out together in unison a song that sounds like a praise to God as one listens to it. In heaven, his creation will show its praise of God at different times. In heaven, there are soft breezes, and in these breezes a sound comes forth saying beautiful words and music about God.

"It's all here, Felicia!" Wee Angel said as she jumped up and down.

She spotted a special fruit. The name was like a pineapple and the taste close to it too! Wee Angel quickly picked one for Felicia and handed it to her.

Both spotted a large rock they could sit upon! In fact, this rock was large enough that both had to use their wings and fly a few feet up to its top.

Once seated they were busy eating this fruit, it was like a banana in size and length. It grew from a bush in the forest.

"Wow!" Felicia spoke, "It does taste like a pineapple."

So both sat and ate on this rock. The trees were similar to redwoods on earth.

There were some rocks on the forest floor and mighty pretty flowers. Sir William grazed off the path as he enjoyed some small herb plants by some tree trunks.

Wee Angel said, "Felicia, we can walk on this golden path, then there is a clearing, and then some meadows, and then.... the pond. From there we enter some more woods and we will come to a hillside, then a clearing. Finally a small hill and then there is a very special rock."

For the moment though, they were busy with the fruit.

Now another friend of Wee Angel's and Sir William came through the trees.

His name was Benjamin. He was a beautiful elk with large beautiful antlers, and with him was Bell, a tall ostrich.

Both came to Felicia and greeted her in their heavenly way. A nice hug!

Then down the path through the woods to this special rock walked Felicia, Wee Angel and their friends.

They hadn't walked far when they met James and Angel Michael. Everyone greeted everyone. One had to remember that since Wee Angel was so little, she was very special to many of the angels and saints.

Wee Angel told them they were going to the special rock.

James and Angel Michael said they had come to the forest for prayer, but they would love to go with everyone.

Felicia said, "My! Am I blessed to have them with!"

Wee Angel said, "Now Felicia, they are busy, but God tells them they have to help, and be with us little ones too!"

James prayed out loud so all would listen to him as he spoke praises!

Angel Michael was quiete. He liked it that way at times. He picked up Wee Angel and carried her on his shoulder, but that didn't go too far until Felicia asked the same. Angel Michael had to carry both.

Angel Michael could change his size if he had too, because of his great power. God gave that gift to him.

After quite some time they came to the edge of the forest and continued on the golden path through the meadows.

Soon they met Karen and Sue. They joined the others.

There were other golden paths that joined this one. A couple of birds came and sat on the back of Sir William, a cardinal and a couple of blue jays. Above everyone some swallows kept up their flight. Felicia asked if she could lead everyone.

James said, "Go ahead, my child, take the lead."

And lead, Felicia did, as she walked up in front of everyone! Soon a few more horses that were in a small pasture area joined the others.

As they walked, six more sisters and brothers joined in with them.

Wee Angel being close to Felicia spoke to everyone, "See that pond ahead, it's so pretty!"

It wasn't big, but it was very beautiful!

Soon they were by it. What made it so pretty was the three streams that came into this one pond. All around it were roses, different colored roses.

Michael said, "How much Jesus loves roses!"

Each stream had to go over a small waterfall before the water splashed into the pond. The surroundings were perfect.

As they looked back from there they saw the beautiful forest. All around them were groupings of bushes, very low to the grass. There were flowers of different sizes. The Creator cared about the little as much as he cared about the vast.

The pond was about a stone's throw in size. In the middle were a couple of pelicans. Around the sides some long legged type birds walked and enjoyed everything.

The setting was perfect.

As they stood looking at the pond, three angels with instruments landed by them. One had a violin, one had a flute, and the other could sing. They started playing and the one started to sing to them. The songs were songs of prayer.

They played and sang a few songs, and after prayers, they were in the sky to another place to play for others.

Wee Angel said to Felicia, "We should be going!"

Felicia agreed and told all the others. She got out in front to lead them.

Angel Michael and James had the biggest smiles watching, as Felicia and Wee Angel were doing their best to get everyone together.

Chapter 11

Onward

Bell the ostrich seemed to get a lot of attention by everyone. Benjamin the elk was so majestic. He had such a special look that everyone was in awe of his beauty.

Sue, rode on his back for a while.

He enjoyed carrying passengers if it wasn't too far for him.

Karen pointed out a cloud to Felicia, "Look! Look at the colors on the underside of the cloud."

"Yes," Felicia replied, "They are again like a rainbow."

A saint on a horse came from the opposite direction. He told everyone that they weren't too far from the rock.

Soon they were entering another forest of trees. These were all pine trees. All were very straight.

"My, Oh my!" Felicia exclaimed, "What a pleasant fragrance."

Many of the sisters and brothers again had some tears of joy as they looked at the tree and smelled the tree's fragrance. Of course, the pines were a home to many little ones of God's. His squirrels, chipmunks, raccoons, owls, eagles, heavenly land squirrels, deer, rabbits, bears, and many more animals that are not on earth.

The golden path would wind and curve through the woods, but soon they came to open land.

This land was where the special rock was that so many came and saw, it's beauty.

It was beauty in a different way! In the Bible God opened a rock for drink!

Felicia and Wee Angel were still walking in the front and Karen was close by them.

Then the others followed including Benjamin, Sir William and Bell. Just outside the forest was Beth who was like our australian sheepdog.

She joined and immediately ran up to Felicia and Wee Angel to be greeted!

The land was very pasture-like with heavy thick, but short grass. One saw a couple of streams, as one looked in different directions.

In front of them it was getting more hilly.

In fact, there was a flock of sheep grazing to the right side of the path as they continued on towards the rock.

The golden path was slowly going upwards a little and all around them were very plush hills, so gentle in slope, so rich! There were no trees in the area.

Then ahead of them on the side of the hill, almost at the top of the hill was a large rock.

The rock was about four lengths of a man tall, three lengths of a man for it's width, and about three lengths of man in it's depth.

Out of the rock about two-thirds up from the bottom and in the center water was gushing out of it. It gushed out from the inside of the rock.

It was the only rock on the hillside, in fact, as one looked in all directions there wasn't another rock.

The sheep on the hillside went about their grazing.

Above this, there was a special serenity as Felicia, Wee Angel, and others looked at it.

Felicia quietly said, "You know it reminds me of Jesus when he gave us the Beatitudes and multiplied the fish, bread, and how he spoke on the hillside to the 5,000. The Word never stopped flowing from him as the waters are doing here."

Above them the heavenly skies were the most beautiful blues and around them was the most rich greens. Evenly in height was the grass.

As they stood others were coming there.

Golden paths went off into different directions so many could come and enjoy this. The stream slowly flowed out and around the hills and that in itself was special for all of them to watch as the waters flowed away from it and on, and on, and on and..........on!

Michael told them the rock kept gushing out the water and never stopped!

James led everyone in prayer and they praised God the Father!

Angel Michael had to be leaving so he bid each one good-day and was off into the heaven's sky.

Chapter 12

To the Canyon

After they watched Angel Michael fly away, it wasn't long that everyone started to go on their own way.

Wee Angel and Felicia decided to climb unto the back of Sir William and fly for a while.

They bid good-days to everyone including James, Benjamin, Bell, and Beth.

Then into the heavenly sky, Sir William flew with the two on his back. Wee Angel said they should go to the Glory Canyons.

She said it was quite a distance, so they made themselves comfortable for the ride.

After some heavenly time both were getting hungry and tired besides, so they told Sir William to land near an orchard of many varieties of fruit.

Land, he did, with gentleness and grace!

Both, jumped off of his back. The orchard was next to a field with many grapevines.

It had peaches, pears, bananas, apples, plums, apricots, cherries, and much more.

They told Sir William to graze for a while!

Both flew and climbed in the trees, picked what they needed for themselves.

Heaven was not without vegetables. They are there too!

Felicia and Wee Angel had found some tomatoes.

Wee Angel said, "Now, I have to share some tidbits of knowledge for you, Felicia. On earth, the body is made up of flesh, but in heaven, it has light in it. So do the vegetables and fruit! It's the light in it that we use, whether we need it, I don't know, but we can enjoy the fruits and vegetables. I understand very little about this, but I know everything is sweetened just right to our taste! The life of all things comes from God the Father."

For the most part, the fields were pretty flat!

They had flown over many of them (all plush), rivers, streams, gentle rolling hills, pastures, lakes, no mountains though! As before, when finished with eating, they were tired, so both found a spot and slept!

Remember, there are no bugs and the temperature was always just right for the saints, angels, God's animals, and birds.

Even Sir William rested close by the two as they slept after their meal.

After the two woke up they sat and talked!

They talked about heaven and how beautiful it was, and about God's creation.

"Wee Angel," Felicia quietly said, "As I look at the grapevines, these trees, his big and little flowers, shrubs, grass, all the places we've been, all the saints, all the angels we've seen, I'm so thankful to be here!"

Felicia prayed and ended her prayer, "Thank you, Jesus for loving Wee Angel! Thank you for loving me!"

Wee Angel added, "We've only been to a few places. God's creation goes on, and on, and on!

Wee Angel finally said to Felicia that they should be going on again!

So on again, they went on Sir William.

They just kept crossing field after field, trees and more trees, streams and more streams. They also saw many saints on the golden paths headed to their destinations as well!

They have met on the paths and have flown over many saints, who were enjoying heaven.

After time(heaven's time), they saw in the distance some mighty canyons. The fields bordering the canyons were rolling hills, nothing jagged or rugged in appearance.

Above the canyons was light that again had the glory to it. Brilliant, radiance of colors in the sky, high above the canyons below this. They were on the high side of the canyons which had rivers that flowed slowly and peacefully in the bottom.

The colors of the canyon rocks and stones were yellow-oranges, but very light in color. There always was that heavenly radiance, even the canyons! There were no shadows like earth. Everything, very alive, in color and beauty!

Pretty soon they landed, fairly close to a level place by the canyon.

Felicia and Wee Angel walked on one of the paths going up to the rim, where others were viewing the majestic canyon.

The river was quite a distance down the sloping walls. It glistened and sparkled of pure waters!

"Oh my!" said Felicia, "Look there!"

On the opposite wall of the canyon was the image of a cross.

"Isn't that special?" Wee Angel added.

The cross was very large on the canyon side. It was like a separate type of stone laid into the canyon wall. The cross also glistened with extra radiance!

As one looked to the right side of the cross, was a waterfall, with its waters going down a long distance to the river.

The canyon was a part of this river and other rivers that entered into it.

Rolling hills were on the other side with areas of trees.

Far to the right, as they looked, again were some mountains, tall mountains with snow on their peaks.

Sir William was not short of attention as many other saints were grooming or talking to him as one would talk to a horse.

They were just about ready to leave after visiting with some of the saints when a little girl walked up to

Felicia. She asked if she could have a ride to the orchestra as she was a member.

The little girl who was taller than Felicia said she played the violin.

Then Felicia asked, "What is your name?"

Felicia seemed to know her.

"My name is Bernette."

"Bernette! Oh my! Oh my!" Felicia went on, "I'm so glad to see you."

Wee Angel was introduced, but she knew Bernette. She knew Felicia and her were going to talk awhile

since they had known each other on earth.

So on and on, Bernette and Felicia talked, and talked........ and talked!

Finally Wee Angel said, "We can take you Bernette, but I will have to fly."

Wee Angel flew next to Sir William and talked to the saints about their plans. Everyone said their good-days! Many times the good-days included prayers and praises to the Lord as each one was given the gift for thankfulness the moment they came into God's heaven.

Chapter 13

To the Concert

In heaven, there were no strong gusts of wind, no thunderstorms, so flying was always smooth and comfortable, for everyone, including the horses.

Then as they were flying another horse flew to them with a passenger, Aaron said he was going to the same place, so he and his horse named Joan flew with them.

They flew somewhat in the same direction that they had come from! They headed to another very pretty area of trees.

Sir William and Joan kept flying, flying, and flying!

Felicia called to Wee Angel, "How much further is it?"

"Not too far now!" answered Wee Angel, "Just over that ridge we have coming ahead. Then we can see the trees!"

After a moment or two, "There they are!" exclaimed the jubilant, Felicia.

It wasn't much more then a few minutes, Sir William and Joan, landed so gracefully.

The forest wasn't to huge, but the trees were! Here the trees were huge around the outside. The orchestra hall was in one of them, hollowed out, at the base of the tree.

Amongst the trees was grass for animals, including the horses. There were golden paths coming and going from this hall. The other trees had hallowed out rooms as well at the base of the trunk.

Some were for prayers, others for visiting, and with tables. The doorway to the orchestra hall was doubled with a cross over the top of the doorway.

Bernette said she would see them after the concert. She told them she had to hurry inside. She was to play the violin. So after the hugs, she left Wee Angel and Felicia outside.

They looked at the rows and rows of flowers around the orchestra hall and up the sides of the tree grew vines, not too many, just right!

They soon walked inside and the first thing Felicia said, "My, Oh my! Look at the lights, I've never seen anything like this!"

Wee Angel explained them to Felicia, "They are candles that have soft glowing flames on them." For all around the sides of the hall theses candles were set into the wood, hundreds of them. The flames were so appealing, yet soft glowing, and they never had to be put out. They glowed all the time!

Wee Angel whispered to Felicia, "Oh yes, they cannot cause a fire. God made sure of that!"

All the sides of the hall were wood, but not rough wood. It had the grains of a tree, and it was polished out like the furniture on earth. Inlaid into the wood were special gems that glistened. The gems were placed close by each candle so that the light would sparkle through them.

The ceiling was smooth the same way, and inlaid in the ceiling were little designs of crosses by more gems.

The gems on the sides varied in colors, but the gems on the ceiling were all of a light green to light blue color.

Some gems were large, some gems were very small. The crosses were all the same size.

Felicia said, "Aren't those crosses beautiful, Wee Angel?"

"Yes! God told us he did little things like that for those that carried a cross for him on earth. He said it's his way of thanking them!"

The gems scattered the light of the candles to give everything a warm and a feeling of awe. There was plenty of light, no darkness.

Wee Angel said to Felicia, "Go down to the front..."

Felicia did and she was given a flute to play. The director said she could play meaning if she never played a flute before, she could now!

Felicia took a seat with the children's orchestra and, of course, she had to wave to Wee Angel who had a big smile on her face, seated towards the back of the hall. The place was filled with saints, children, and some angels.

After prayer, praise, and thanksgiving to God, the orchestra started to play glories, and hallelujah's to God.

As the concert was finishing up, Bernette went over to Felicia, and gave her a big hug.

Everyone joined in prayer before leaving the concert hall.

Of course, Felicia and Bernette cried with joy, in seeing each other again in their new home, heaven!

Both knew they would be seeing each other many times.

Wee Angel told Bernette she was showing Felicia a few places in heaven.

Both said their good-days.

They were all smiles. They felt so much love, peace and joy.

After the waving, Wee Angel and Felicia walked alongside of Sir William, talked about Bernette, and the concert.

Chapter 14

Some Little Friends

Wee Angel walked alongside of Sir William and continued along a path in the forest further into the woods.

They were so joyful at heart! Felicia had seen much in heaven. Her heavenly time had been well spent and she felt so happy inside.

Wee Angel continued to tell her about the other places in heaven that in heavenly time they would see, but she wanted Felicia to enjoy each moment and not be rushed in any way.

She said heaven was so vast and that one could not understand it all because of this vastness. They walked next to some large rocks and enjoyed the beauty of the forest.

Again the plushness of the flowers upon the forest floor was so enduring to the heart of Felicia.

She walked off the path and picked flowers, picked them one at a time, then held it up and said, "God, thank you! Thank you for making this flower. Thank you, Jesus."

She felt so much praise and thank you's in her heavenly heart, that she had to get them out, as she held the flowers.

These looked like violets with their glistening petals and stems.

Heaven again being celestial, the light seemed to pass through the petals and flowers making them more glowing to the heavenly eyes. Wee Angel showed Felicia how she could on some see her hand on the back side of the flower.

The thick carpet-like floor of the forest was easy to walk upon and the forest floor was not covered in any way with debris or dead limbs. Only life, all was alive with the inner glow given to each as the Creator breathed upon the most perfect of his creation.

Wee Angel, of course, looked at the flowers as well, and Sir William didn't seem to mind at all being in the forest.

Wee Angel added, “We've seen so much!”

They continued along on the golden path.

Felicia soon said with excitement, “I've just got to fly a little more!”

So off she flew around some of the trees with their straight trunks.

She still wasn't the best at it for she would tip too much or land too quickly!

But Wee Angel said she would soon know how without any problems.

Wee Angel pointed with her arm, “See Felicia! Look through the trees. See in the distance the mountains with the many falls! See Felicia!”

“Yes, I see them! Oh my!” again the words came out!

“See! Felicia, the trees are so placed that one could see far between them. We will get to the mountains, sometime! They are mountains that have many small streams coming down and then there are many waterfalls, all in a row. All about the same height, but all separate making up the row of falls.

The water comes down oh so very gently!” Wee Angel explained.

“Oh my!” again said Felicia, “I love how one can look so far through the trees and yet the trees are so full with leaves. The floor of the forest is so plush!”

Wee Angel pointed to many of the different flowers and talked a little about them.

The birds were singing and some would come right down by Felicia's feet and then looked at her.

They didn't look to be fed, but it was their way of saying or greeting one in heaven.

They just loved being there.

Then Wee Angel said, “Felicia, now reach down and touch the robin.”

“He doesn't move, Wee Angel. He likes me to touch him.”

“Yes!” said Wee Angel. “They like to be touched and they come close, you can touch them if you would like, and they will stand for you. Then, when you're done they'll fly away! Felicia, only a few will come to you at a time. It's seems, it's the way God has told them.”

“That's wonderful, Wee Angel!” as Felicia continued to touch the little birds.

Others on the limbs flew closer, watched, sang their heavenly songs to Felicia and Wee Angel.

“They are not scared of us. Oh my!”

Other little ones came closer to them.

There were rabbits, squirrels, chipmunks, raccoons, and others. Of course, Wee Angel had to say to Felicia that the Lord would often tell her while watching Felicia on earth,”Wee Angel, now take extra special care of Felicia. She is so much like a little rabbit. She's shy and she just likes to run...”

“So I would giggle, but I found out he was right.”

Felicia said, “Thank you, Wee Angel for caring, thank you!” Both giggled together for they indeed enjoyed themselves.

The forest was alive with God's little ones.

“Wee Angel, there seems to be so many!”

Soon they walked again with Sir William. After going around hills of trees and through areas where the forest was flat, they came to a meadow.

Both danced and praised the Lord, and both hugged Sir William. Oh heaven was kind! It spoke kindness and love to their very being!

They talked and as they talked, again some more tears came to their eyes.

As far as they could see away from the forest were hills, mountains, and some waterfalls from a stream that was close by them. In the distance, they could still see the mountains with the many falls in a row.

Wee Angel said, "Let's go there now, I can't wait until another time. Angel Michael said I could take you there on this trip if I wanted to for you!"

Both got on Sir William and soon he flew just above the meadows to another place in God's heaven.

Chapter 15

To the Falls and A Glorious Sight

Sir William flew along with ease while Wee Angel and Felicia whistled to their hearts content.

This time a little sparrow flew up to them and soon sat on the back of Sir William with them. Of course, they kept whistling and soon the sparrow joined in with them to the melodies of heaven.

The little sparrow hopped on Felicia's lap for a while, sang some more, then nodded it's head, and flew towards a large tree.

As they looked towards the many falls, the rainbows filled the heaven's skies with golden glories above the mountains, made them know this was a special place.

Wee Angel told Sir William to fly up past the falls to the upper side of the streams.

Soon, they approached and many other saints were there, too!

They landed and greeted others.

They stood and looked at the trees next to the streams, before the waters started on their descent to the base of the mountains.

The streams went over the sides, separate, and they looked like fingers as the streams came from a larger river divided by rocks. There were mountain sides that went much higher yet, to the sides of the falls. There were twelve separate streams here, from one river and Wee Angel told Felicia just around some bends were more streams and falls. All were about the same level across the mountains sides. From where they stood, they saw down the mountain over some hills, meadows and forests that they had come from earlier.

In the distance, some bursts of light occurred above the heavenly horizon.

Wee Angel said, "Oh! That's a part of God's glory over and by his city. When we travel away from the city, it seems no mater how far away we are from it, that at moments by looking in the heavenly sky we can still see these bursts of light. Many colors, and they are not always the same. The colors of the rays are the radiance of his glory, and the bursts of light can vary in brightness, but always one stands in awe of them!"

"Of my!" Felicia spoke again, "Oh my! I've never seen anything like that...."

That's all she said as tears filled her eyes.

Both enjoyed God's beauty as they looked across the valley, hills, meadows, and forests that were below them. They stood by Sir William at the top of the river that formed the twelve falls.

In the distance, they watched a group of angels flying just above the meadows.

Wee Angel said, "They always fly together. God made them that way. There are other groups like this that stay together in whatever God wants of them."

Felicia enjoyed how they looked so beautiful as they flew across a stream and a small cluster of trees in the meadows.

They were flying and then they turned and started to fly towards Wee Angel and Felicia.

As they got closer, the lead angel waved to them and directed the others to stand in a row. \All in front of Wee Angel and Felicia.

Felicia by now, had to count them!

Thirty three angels stood all in one row. All about the same height.

Then the leader angel said, "We came to sing some choruses. My name is Gideon. Angel Michael said Felicia is royalty! I must find you and that we must sing to you!"

They sang a special "Welcome to Heaven song," to Felicia.

She was in tears and happy with graciousness. Felicia enjoyed it!

It was a beautiful sight to see, thirty three angels sang to Felicia, Wee Angel and Sir William. Other saints stood by the streams that cascaded to the valleys below!

Soon they flew into heaven's sky on another errand for Angel Michael.

Sir William by now gained his own crowd of brothers and sisters admiring his beauty.

He always enjoyed it.

After awhile Wee Angel and Felicia climbed aboard Sir William. He walked along the stream further up the mountain.

The bursts of light that were streaming in the sky had slowed, but their heavenly hearts hadn't yet gotten over everything.

Every now and then Wee Angel flew up and away to pick special blue mountain flowers. She even brought some berries for them.

It was nap time again for them and Sir William needed the rest too!

The fragrance of the air was so fresh to them. As they woke, they had another surprise.

"Tuddley Teddy!" both Wee Angel and Felicia exclaimed together as they ran to him and another bear that was with him.

"Everybody just calls him Berry and his name spoke for itself as to why!" said Wee Angel.

Berry was about the same size as Tuddley, but a deeper brown color.

After all the hugs and greetings, which included Sir William, Wee Angel and Felicia each said a prayer.

Then they walked again, talked, sang, looked at various animals, birds and thanked God!

Even some mountain sheep came up to them and walked with them. It was quite a sight, an angel, Felicia, a horse with wings, two bears, and some mountain sheep.

Other saints joined in and walked with them, all enjoyed the views of the hills on the lower sides of the mountains.

John, one of the saints, said they should rest in an open area ahead of them.

Again it was special to see everyone resting! Even a few birds came to sing to them.

A large collie dog named Betsy joined them. A raccoon stopped, and played a little while, then an owl landed close by, even a cougar came and slept by the sheep. Out of the woods came a few more bear and in time one of the saints suggested they sing a few gospel songs.

Tuddley Teddy was busy after he woke, as he received more hugs from the saints.

Felicia and Wee Angel played and gave hugs to all the animals.

Soon Wee Angel said they should be going in the heavenly sky. Again they gave hugs to Tuddley and others.

Felicia whispered to Tuddley, "I can't wait to see you again! We'll be back!"

Soon in the heavenly sky Sir William flew with them on his back. He flew just above the trees. They made a couple of large circles so they could see everyone on heaven's land.

Sir William flew back towards the valleys of the mountains to the next place for them.

Felicia in her heart made some beautiful friends with many saints, she had met as well as God's little ones.

She was so thankful for everything and whispered to Wee Angel, "My heart is full of joy! The joy of heaven is everything the Bible said it would be!"

Chapter 16

A Place of Prayer

It wasn't long as Sir William flew with his wings moving up and down that seven other winged horses with saints joined them in flight.

A sight it was as these beautiful horses flew above the tree tops.

As Felicia saw all the riders, the Lord discerned to her of what she had learned while on earth.

She quickly thought how majestic they will look as they fly through heaven's door to the horizons of earth. She thought how the armies with their electronic weapons will be standing under a false leadership commanded by the enemy to heaven.

Oh! What a majestic sight that will be as they battle and stand and then up over the horizons of earth in the sky will come the Commander-in-Chief of heaven riding upon a white winged horse with his riders.

Oh the shock on the faces of those in this place as so stated by the Bible.

She knew that Sir William was going to be in this battle. She knew as she rode upon his back that he was going to be in it. She whispered this to Wee Angel. She nodded her head in agreement.

Of course, Sir William was always just a little larger then the other horses.

One of the saints said to Wee Angel that they should follow them.

They flew around curves, bends, mountain sides, over streams, as they were still in the mountains. They viewed other horses with riders.

Soon all the horses landed on the path, one at a time.

Then, of course, everyone talked a little, and on they went! Soon they walked between two hills of the mountains where the sides went up very sharply above them. They enjoyed the columns of greens laid over the rock formations.

Many types of vines and grass with flowers of various colors on them. Soon they went through a fairly narrow way with these cliff-like rocks on sides.

They came to a more open area still with the steepness of the sides rising above them.

Here all the animals had to be left for this special place was not for them.

They walked through more cliff-like walkways then they came to a huge open area with the hills rising very sharply around it.

They saw many saints in prayer there.

Many dressed in white raiment. Even the garments were not made like the ones on earth. They always stayed clean!

They listened as the sounds of their prayers filled the heavenly air.

Hundreds and hundreds of saints in prayer.

They came and went as they felt led by the spirit of the Lord.

Around the sides angels sang praises to God. At the top of the cliff-like area, were several rows of angels all the way around the prayer area. These angels had an instrument or horn that at the same time they would stand and sound a heavenly sound. This they did at various intervals of time!

Up and above in the sky, glories of light flowed upward, with flying or hovering angels that were always there.

Wee Angel told Felicia those angels were very special, because they could be that way and are a part of God's glory.

The sounds of the voices filled the heavenly air, then the horns would blow!

At times the angels in the glory light that went upward as high as their heavenly eyes could see, would break out in songs of praise and worship.

The glories of light were always there!

Saints stood praying, raised arms and hands praising, many knelt praying, and others prayed face down.

At times they all stood and praised together in the heavenly language.

More horns blew and the sounds rang upwards!

Wee Angel and Felicia felt the awesome power of prayer as it filled the air.

Both joined in the praises. Then after a time, they walked out as others came and left at all times.

Wee Angel told Felicia this was just one of the special prayer places.

They walked Sir William through the hillsides and soon they came to a clearing where they climbed on his back. They gave Sir William the yes to fly, and they soon were in flight again!

They felt so blessed on being able to be a part of worshiping and praying to God in his heaven. They loved the joy of heaven!

Chapter 17

A Special Blessing

Wee Angel said to Felicia, “I'm going to have Sir William fly to a special place.” “They're all very special.” answered Felicia.

“Yes, but this is very special in a totally different way.”

They relaxed on Sir William's back as he kept flying, flying.... and flying!

Sir William flew much quicker than before!

Soon they landed by a tall area of trees, as they had flown more to open land where there were many fields of grass. Many types of green grass that were of different shades.

It looked like a quilt from the sky with many different squares of green. The grass was always beautiful, as before, the same length, and easy to walk on!

Besides the fields had a beautiful glow to them as they looked from the back of Sir William. The trees were in a small grouping. They journeyed for quite a ways, and a rest couldn't have come at a better time.

They saw deer, antelope, and again some grazing animals that are not on earth.

The skies were very open here. The surroundings seemed to talk to their heart and soul. On the horizon they saw more bursting of light from God's city. It quickly touched their feelings and their heavenly heart.

“Felicia,” Wee Angel spoke up, “We'll walk from here. We are just about to arrive at some hills and that's where we will see what I want to share with you.”

There was a golden path, not too far from them, and after a rest the three were on their way. Wee Angel and Felicia looked at the open spaces. It was like the plains as on earth except they did not have as rich a grass as was here in heaven.

God did this for a reason as they walked on to a surprise. On the path, they met many other saints that were going in the same direction. All were excited, and yet, were very humble about the moment. Felicia knew as they met others, the specialness of this moment.

Onward they walked and the hills started to get closer. At first very small hills, but as they walked further the hills were even taller.

Pretty soon in the distance, they walked over a hill, and there it was!

It was a very......very...... very.... large cross!

“Oh my!” Felicia said, “My, how large it is!”

“Yes, very large and high! The cross is at least three very tall heavenly trees high,” with humility Wee Angel explained, “the angels put the cross up for everyone. They did it as a remembrance of what Jesus had gone through for man and also everyone in heaven as they came to Jesus. The angels kept saying to God, 'Can't we do something because of what happened and what is happening on earth.'”

“God said they could put this up for a remembrance for us. He said to put it up in a open area so many could come, see it, and feel how it stands out and away from others. Yet, each had to take that step.”

They saw many special benches on all sides on heaven's grass.

The grass was even shorter as they neared the cross.

The cross stood high above all the saints. As they walked withing the special area with many benches, not like ours on earth, a beautiful feeling occurred to them. All of a sudden, they saw more angels. There were all around the cross and again a glory light was present there. They heard music, and melodies that were sung on earth about the cross.

Some of the angels played different instruments. They were all in the glorious light in the heavenly sky. There were songs like "The Old Rugged Cross and Amazing Grace" and many more!

The angels sang some, spoke some, and some just instrumentals.

Then light, glorious light beamed all around!

All the time the benches were pretty much filled with saints, many in prayer. Some praised our Lord and thanked our Lord, but all so very humble. Wee Angel and Felicia said a prayer. Then as they walked away from there, they couldn't see the angels or hear the music, but they saw the cross stand above everything, stand out there on heaven's land.

Neither said a word as they looked at it. Both stood and looked and looked!

They stood silent for a time.

Then without a word they flew on Sir William's back and soon he flew again! Felicia and Wee Angel had their eyes glued on the cross as they kept looking at it from heaven's sky.

What a beautiful sight as all the paths led up to it from all directions!

Both pondered and pondered!

Both knew what it meant!

Sir William turned his head, Wee Angel gave him the signal and told him where to head next! He turned his head and with majestic grace and quietness, flew on!

Felicia was overwhelmed by the beauty of the cross.

Onward Sir William flew, their hearts filled with a new joy and a new love. Always that special inner feeling to the son of God who went to the cross for all mankind.

Chapter 18

Back to God's City

It wasn't long and Sir William landed!

Wee Angel and Felicia decided to walk for a while and Sir William followed behind them.

“I have sure seen a lot!” said Felicia.

“Yes, but it never stops here, Felicia.”

They had landed on heaven's ground where the grass was short and plush.

Not far from them were ponds, marshlands with tall reeds, cattails, but these in heaven, are not stagnant as on earth. There was fresh clear water flowing into it, and constantly out of it. No dead reeds, everything was alive and green. Still, heaven had the redwing blackbirds as on earth, as other birds that liked to sit on the reeds of a pond.

Felicia looked into the waters and again said, “I can't get over how clear and pure these waters are!”

The bottom of the pond had pretty crystals instead of mud that often were in ponds on earth.

It was rest time again for the two, and rest they did, as they stretched out, and slept on the grass.

Soon they awoke to a large white bear close by them. Wee Angel said he was like a polar bear, but he didn't need the snow.

His fur was still very cuddly as the two played with him.

Soon they walked on the trail and enjoyed everything. They were getting closer to some higher hills and by sight some mountains in the distance. Then another angel came to them.

He had been flying pretty fast so they thought it must be important.

The angel said they should head back to the city of God's dwelling and there be greeted with a message.

Felicia praised the Lord as she looked at everything around her.

Yes, there were reeds and ponds, but off in the short distance were some hills with a stream that ran through them that had several waterfalls. The sky again had many birds flying and a couple of saints on winged horses.

The fragrance of the air was fresh and clean. They were close by a few white daises.

Between the hills and mountains were more trees of medium height. The other direction the heaven's land was slightly rolling with groupings of trees, the clouds high and light in size.

The white bear had decided to go his way. He joined up with some more bears, some were white, and some were brown.

It seemed like all of them were headed for a berry patch that they discovered by some bushes and shrubs.

Wee Angel said, "Oh yes, God has plants instead of honey hives where the bears can eat so there are no bees. The honey seems to grow on a plant so they always have some, because bears seem to eat and eat...... and eat this honey.

Wee Angel and Felicia rode on Sir William's back. He walked and followed the golden path through the hills and then along the bottom of some mountains. They followed the winding path, meeting other saints with horses, other brothers, sisters, and children.

They stopped and talked to some saints for heaven's length of time.

Along the way, they spotted more deer, a dog or two, a cat or two, an ox, a camel, even a large tiger(very tame, you know), a moose and others. Soon they saw the majestic city. It was not short of glorious colors. It had all the colors and brilliant colors of gems. It had radiance, and it had glorious colors above it and all around in the sky. It was and is what it is, a dwelling place of God!

At a distance the sky showed the glories of this city. The buildings were the same way. Everything was pure without blemish! Waterfalls and streams went through parts of the city. Special trees that were no other place in heaven or on earth. There were bushes that glowed and burned like the burning bush where God spoke to Moses.

Gems that are only in this city and no place else.

The streets were paved the same way, the finest gold, unique in this being the only city with it! Some of the gates have special gems!

Remember the glories of light gave off a golden hue around whatever one looked at with heavenly eyes. On earth one saw shadows, but in heaven around anything was a little glow. Heaven was

celestial with light.

The city was even above this in it's light because of God's glories and power!

Everything in the city was different from all else. Waters that seemed like they glowed with the finest soft fire inside the water.

Woods that were so carefully picked and polished. It was, what it was, a dwelling place for God's authority and for those that are chosen to see him.

Felicia and Wee Angel left Sir William outside the gate and walked into the city. Soon a messenger told them they were to go to a special service in heaven. They were so excited!

Wee Angel said, “I want to show you something, Felicia!”

So off they walked to this place in the city.

Soon they came and entered another courtyard, a very large, court yard.

As they walked through the gates, they saw another wall, but this wall was made of canvas, and had ropes on it with an entrance. Felicia knew this was like the tabernacle grounds as in the Old Testament.

DANIEL

Wee Angel said, "We can't go into the Holy of Holies, but we can enjoy it from here and remember we can go see God now as we have seen him! It's special, isn't it, Felicia?"

"It is!" whispered Felicia with more tears in her eyes. "It's so special! It's so special!"

Wee Angel went on, "God made this like the one he had man make for him."

Felicia said, "Think of it, Wee Angel, God being almighty and us being so finite. He did everything to have us love him as he loves us. He sent his son to do the same for us. Jesus helped us come even closer to him as the Father and the Holy Spirit as the dove to carry out everything between God and man."

"Isn't he wonderful?" said Felicia with more tears. "Isn't he wonderful?"

They sat on the grounds and cried over its beauty for they knew it was close to God's heart.

After heaven's time, they walked back through the entrance, and left this special place in the city where God dwells!

They greeted others, and soon walked out of the city to find Sir William.

Chapter 19

A Special Service

Felicia was impressed and in such joy about heaven and now she was going to a very special service there.

As Sir William flew over heaven's land, Felicia noticed his quiet and ever faithful way of doing exactly what one asked him.

The animals had no rebellion in them.

In the distance they saw a place where the heaven's sky above the area had a special glow of glory.

There were first flat lands, with fields of flowers. There were fields of lilies, fields of tulips, fields of daises, fields of irises, and many more flowers.

They looked from Sir William's back. They saw the outdoor sanctuary for it stretched way to the horizon. They saw gentle rolling hills, and hills that were higher and were a part of the sanctuary. Above this were clouds that were specially feathered and stayed there all the time with glorious colors.

There were paths through the fields of flowers, and hills so that the saints could walk to this sanctuary.

Sir William landed in a special area outside the sanctuary that pastured winged horses and horses for the saints.

Felicia and Wee Angel hugged Sir William. He had become so special to them. They told him that they would see him after service and they told him how they loved him just as children would do!

They followed the others on the golden path that slopped gently upwards and around small hills into larger hills to the open sanctuary.

They came to a gate that was like an archway that was all covered with little roses. They walked through this and into a very large open sanctuary.

From there Wee Angel and Felicia got special seats as did others who had not been to a service like this.

Felicia was overwhelmed in awe!

Once seated, Wee Angel talked to Felicia, “See how God created everything!”

They looked as far as they could see and there were still more seats. The platform was in the middle.

The seats around the sides were created right out of the hills so that the brothers and sisters sat on God made benches with this cushion of small flowers and plants. It took many hills to make the sides. All the way around were levels that were very even. The walls behind each bench from the main floor had a special vine covering with very tiny flowers. All the flowers, vines were very small, plush like a carpet. It was like one cut out these levels from the hills.

After the brothers and sisters, children got their seats, then on the highest rows and above, the angel choir took their places.

All the way to the backside and around like an oval in pattern.

Thousands and thousands and thousands and more all in white garments!

Pretty soon a leader of the choir came out on the platform and he directed the angels to sing! They made the heaven's ring!

Every now and then, the congregation of God's chosen joined in with the singing!

Again they sang songs we know on earth for God's praise and many more!

Pretty soon they started the song, “Jerusalem.”

Wee Angel said to Felicia, “Do you recognize that song?”

Felicia answered, "Yes! The Holy Spirit gave the song to Daniel and I. He said at the time rows and rows of angels were singing it in heaven as far as the eye could see!!" The words were:

JERUSALEM
JERUSALEM
I CALL MY LORD
I CALL MY LORD.

OH PRINCE OF PEACE
OH PRINCE OF PEACE
I CALL HIS NAME
I CALL HIS NAME.

JEHOVAH
JEHOVAH
I CALL MY LORD
I CALL MY LORD.

OH MIGHTY ONE
OH MIGHTY ONE
I CALL HIS NAME
I CALL HIS NAME.

OH SACRED HEART
OH SACRED HEART
I CALL MY LORD
I CALL MY LORD.

HIS MAJESTY
HIS MAJESTY
I CALL HIS NAME
I CALL HIS NAME.

Felicia said to Wee Angel, "They look like they are right out of the Bible."

Wee Angel said softly, “They are!”

“Oh my! Oh my! Felicia kept saying over!

Then she placed her hands on her face.

“Some of the disciples are there, Felicia. Some have other duties. There's also some from the Old Testament and the New Testament. We'll go over their names later.”

Of course, everyone around Felicia and Wee Angel were whispering too!

Soon the choir leader started to have everyone sing a couple more praise songs. And he said they were going to sing the song “Alleluia.”

Wee Angel sang!

Felicia sang!

The congregation sang!

Heaven rang with music and worship!

Both Felicia and Wee Angel had tears flowing down their cheeks.

The joy of heaven was ringing in each one's heart as they all stood in reverence and awe to the feelings God gave them.

Then the choir leader had the music and singing slowly come to a close with a short time of quiet.

Then through a doorway into the sanctuary walked JESUS.

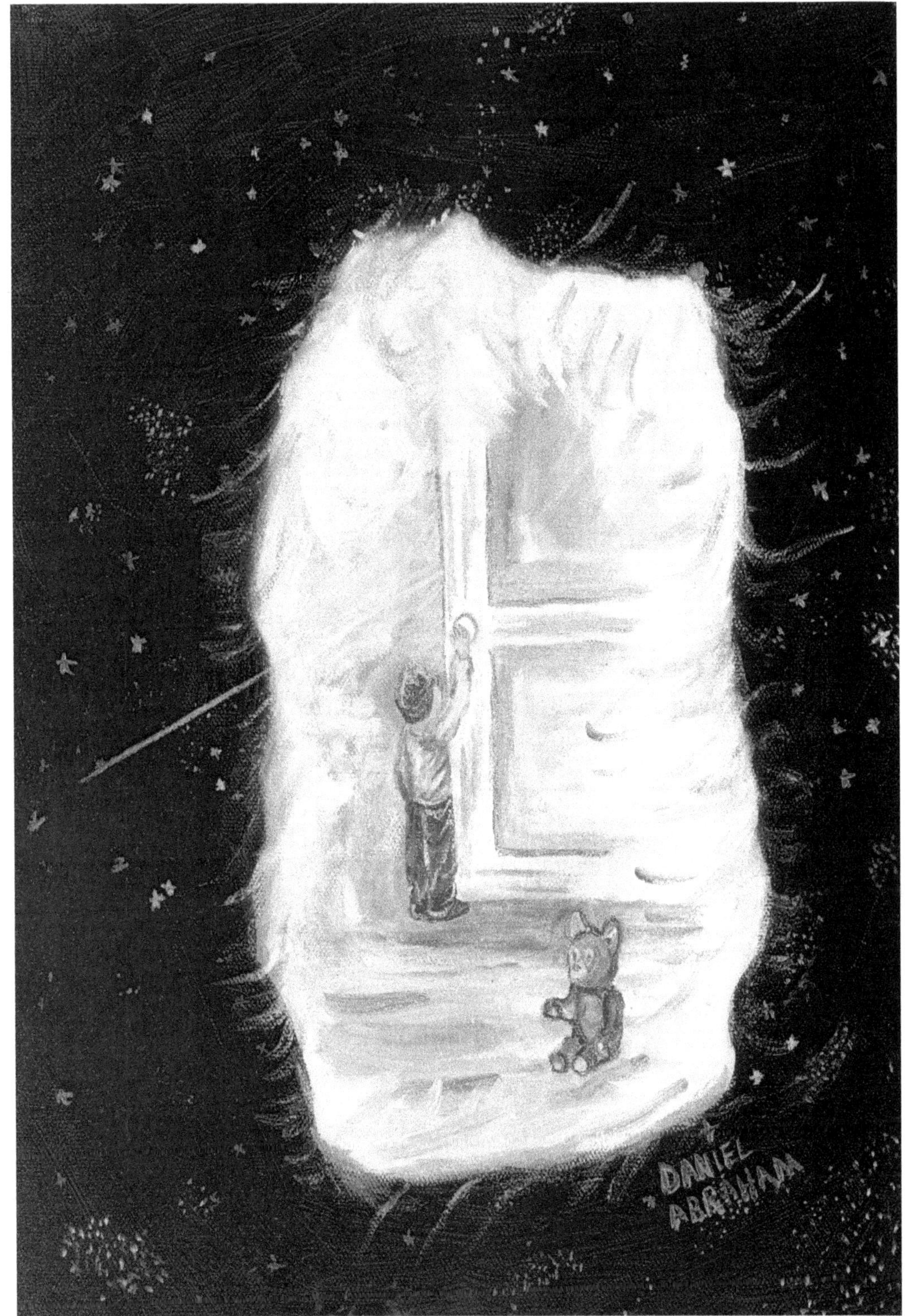
DANIEL
ABRAHAM

Daniel Leske is available for speaking engagements and public appearances. For more information contact:

Daniel Leske
C/O Advantage Books
P.O. Box 160847
Altamonte Springs, FL 32716

info@ advbooks.com

Daniel has also published ***The Joy of Heaven 2*** and ***The Joy of Heaven 3*** available from ***Advantage Books***

To purchase additional copies of this book or other books published by ***Advantage Books*** call our order number at:

407-788-3110 (Book Orders Only)

or visit our bookstore website at: www.advbookstore.com

We are planning to have some children's products of the characters from ***The Joy of Heaven 1, 2,*** and ***3***. They would be stuffed animal toys, teddy bears, figurines, possibly dolls and other products. For more information:

www.thejoyofheaven.com

Facebook: Daniel Leske / Author

Longwood, Florida, USA
"we bring dreams to life"™
www.advbookstore.com

www.ingramcontent.com/pod-product-compliance
Lightning Source LLC
Chambersburg PA
CBHW081518040426
42447CB00013B/3266